Leading from the Lectern

How to Use Meeting Etiquette to
Preside, Facilitate and Shine with
Professionalism and Poise

Special Limited Edition

Sharon Anita Hill, DTM

Leading from the Lectern: How to Use Meeting Etiquette to Preside, Facilitate and Shine with Professionalism and Poise

Other Books by Sharon A. Hill

Wild Woman's Guide to Etiquette: Saving the World One Handshake at a Time

24 Tips for Students to Succeed in College

35 Tips for Students to Succeed in Corporate America

Don't be the Ugly Duckling at the Peacock Party: It's Better to Strut than to Waddle

Acknowledgements

This short guide is a compendium of Toastmasters members' guidelines and tips found on various web sites and in various Toastmasters magazine articles.

Thanks to Paul Gamble and Kathryn Blocksdorf of Barrie Toastmasters, Barrie, Ontario, and Robert A. Richert, DTM, of Helmsman Toastmasters, Fountain Valley, California for permission to use their articles. Thanks to the various contributors throughout the Internet for their etiquette guidelines and tips.

Dedication

What a joy to have like-minded friends share a vision and assist in bringing that vision to fruition. My thanks go to Elmer T. Hill, Joe Novara, Phoenix Miller, and Diana M. Needham for their creative and critical advice.

Leading from the Lectern

How to Use Meeting Etiquette to
Preside, Facilitate and Shine with
Professionalism and Poise

Special Limited Edition

Sharon Anita Hill, DTM

CONTENTS

Other Books by Sharon A. Hill ....

Acknowledgements ....

Dedication ....

Introduction 1

Controlling the Meeting 3

Understanding Lectern Etiquette 5

Approaching and Greeting Your Host 7

Controlling the Lectern 9

Introducing a Speaker 13

Introducing Role Holders 15

Addressing a Lectern Replacement Person 17

Beginning and Ending a Speaking Role 19

Managing Applause 23

Introducing Dignitaries 25

Presenting an Award 29

Accepting an Award 33

Minding Your Manners as an Audience Member 35

    Do's and Don'ts While a Speaker is Speaking 36

Speaking Tips 39

Clichés and Crutch Phrases to Avoid 41

Inducting Club Officers 43

Parliamentary Procedure 49

    Motions 50

Etiquette from Robert A. Richert, DTM (Used with Permission) 53

    First, Lectern or Podium: Which Is It? 54

    Approach the Lectern and Greet Your Host 55

    Control the Lectern 55

Next Success Steps 59

About the Author 61

Introduction

As a seasoned, avid Toastmaster who has attended or participated in hundreds of meetings of all varieties worldwide, it became clear that "we don't know what we don't know" when it comes to presiding, facilitating, and shining as leaders in various settings and situations within the organization.

While meeting etiquette resources are available to all of us online, who has time to research the how-to's when we are filling a critical role in a meeting, especially if it comes as a last-minute request? This short guide is intended to be used as a quick reference so you can always be prepared to step into whatever meeting opportunity arises.

Toastmaster's etiquette is a unique skill each of us as members develop over our tenure of membership in the organization. It is the attention to small details that sets us apart from the average speaker and helps define us as professionals. Good techniques in Toastmasters etiquette create confidence in speakers and bring kudos from audiences. Teaching etiquette at the club level prepares members for success as club ambassadors when they speak beyond the club at other Toastmasters events and outside of the world of Toastmasters.

All Toastmasters clubs have their own culture. For example, some have prepared speeches that precede Table Topics; for Table Topics, some first ask the question, and then select the speaker; others first select the speaker, and then ask the question. This guide strives to be club culture-free and focuses on universal meeting etiquette.

These etiquette rules can be adjusted to meetings outside of Toastmasters. Using the rules will make everyone appear more professional, polished, and confident.

The language of this guide is gender neutral. The word "he" refers to both the masculine and the feminine.

CHAPTER ONE

Controlling the Meeting

Each portion of a Toastmaster's meeting is under the control of one of its key meeting officials: the Presiding Officer, Toastmaster, Table Topics Master or General Evaluator.

Control of a meeting is passed from one official to another by shaking hands when the next key meeting official arrives at the lectern. This is called "passing control of the meeting." Thus, the Presiding Officer passes control to the Toastmaster of the Day who later passes control to the Table Topics Master and then to the General Evaluator. When a key meeting official finishes his portion of the meeting, control is returned to the proper official with a handshake, i.e. control passes from the General Evaluator to the Toastmaster to the Presiding Officer.

Whenever you take control of a meeting, you should acknowledge the person who yields control to you.

CHAPTER TWO

Understanding Lectern Etiquette

There are accepted conventions of meeting protocol that are a part of a well-run meeting. While these conventions may seem overly formal to some people, using them contributes greatly toward a professionally conducted meeting.

- Never leave the lectern unattended. If you are introducing the speaker, after your introduction, wait until the speaker arrives at the lectern. While the Speaker approaches the lectern, applaud him until he arrives.

- Always wait at the lectern until the next speaker arrives. It is poor etiquette to simply pass the speaker, shake hands over the lectern or just nod to him. Shake his right hand as acknowledgment and say a few cordial words of greeting before you walk away. Begin the transition by stepping back to avoid collision as you leave the area.

- When you relinquish control of the lectern, never cross the path or walk in front of the person you are relinquishing control to. The preferred etiquette suggests you step back, away from or pivot and move in the opposite direction of the person who now has control of the lectern.

To ease transition, seating arrangements usually are made prior to the meeting. Speakers are either assigned designated seating or their chairs are placed to the left and right of the lectern so the Toastmaster is able to move and seat himself in either direction. It is preferred that you walk behind the person you relinquish control to, or walk around the perimeter of the audience/room to return to your seat, rather than cross his path.

CHAPTER THREE

Approaching and Greeting Your Host

After you are introduced, don't spend excessive time approaching the lectern. Avoid making side comments to people along the way. Approach in a confident manner and shake hands with your host.

When you carry materials to the lectern, keep your right hand free so you can comfortably shake hands. If both hands are full, put the objects down on or near the lectern and then shake hands. Substantial visual aids should be set up before you are introduced — and prior to the meeting, if possible.

Note: Throughout this guide, the word "host" is used as a generic term for the member who introduces speakers, be it the Toastmaster, Table Topics Master, General Evaluator or whoever fills that role.

CHAPTER FOUR

Controlling the Lectern

When you take control of the lectern, you assume a leadership role. While there, a Toastmaster never appears apologetic. You should be prepared, confident and in charge. Here are some suggested guidelines:

- After you arrive at the lectern and shake hands with your introducer, then turn to the audience members and greet them. The most common greeting is, "Fellow Toastmasters and honored guests…"

- Set everything in your hands on the lectern, such as pens, eyeglasses, notes and other objects. Items you hold are potentially distracting, so unless you intend to begin your speech by displaying one of them, free your hands before you speak.

- Step back a few inches from the lectern to avoid leaning on it.

- Spread your feet to shoulder width so you won't rock back and forth.

- Do not use the gavel. It is for use only by the president or presiding officer.

- Avoid leaving the lectern unattended. In general, Toast-masters etiquette discourages leaving the lectern unattended. However, certain situations may require you to leave the lectern briefly, for example, to help set up visual aids, retrieve an object or in case of an emergency. If you must leave the lectern, always announce your intentions before you go — don't just walk away! If you must leave the lectern for more than a few seconds, declare a brief recess first. Be careful with the terminology: Do not use the word "adjourn" when you mean "recess," because adjourning the meeting means it is over.

- Leave the lectern in good hands. It is never proper for a member to leave the lectern abruptly after speaking. When you are about to relinquish control of the lectern, always:

o   Stay at the lectern until the next person arrives —
    the host, not the next speaker — to take your
    place.

o   Shake hands with that person, pick up your mate-
    rials and then relinquish the lectern.

o   Walk directly back to your seat.

Use the lectern properly to increase meeting efficiency,
help foster a professional atmosphere and promote leadership
training.

CHAPTER FIVE

Introducing a Speaker

In order to establish credibility and prepare the speaker for success, include interesting background points in your introductions:

- Verify his designations (CC, AC, DTM).

- Announce any Toastmasters office he has held.

- Personalize your introduction to warm up the audience.

- Be creative with introductions to pique audience interest in the topic and the speaker.

CHAPTER SIX

Introducing Role Holders

We know the assigned speakers should receive appropriate introductions, but what about the other people in the program? Certainly, the Toastmaster, Table Topics Master and General Evaluator deserve more than mere declarations of their names. These key players deserve introductions, too, although not as comprehensive as those the program speakers do.

Provide the audience with some background information and give them a warm welcome. Here is an example:

"Fellow Toastmasters and most welcome guests, it is my pleasure to introduce one of our club's most active and enthusiastic members. He has been a member of our club for five years and is currently serving as Vice President of Membership. He is a Competent Communicator and last year earned the Advanced Communicator Bronze Award. Please welcome our Toastmaster for the evening, Raymond Doe."

Functionaries and other members who serve in roles may be introduced by title (if a District or Club officer), name and educational award (CC, DTM, etc.). Always be positive and enthusiastic when introducing them.

CHAPTER SEVEN

Addressing a Lectern Replacement Person

It is a fact of life that there will be occasions when the club president, officer, or district dignitary might not be able to attend. In that case, a replacement person will represent them.

Do not address a substitute officer as "Madam Acting President" or "Mr. Presiding Officer." Always identify an officer by his proper title of office: Madam Area Director, Madam President, Mr. Vice-President Education, Mr. Sergeant-at-Arms, etc.

Learn these titles and use them correctly.

CHAPTER EIGHT

Beginning and Ending a Speaking Role

When you begin to speak, first address the person who gave you control.

For example, if you are the Toastmaster and receive control from another meeting official, address the person who gave you control by saying *"Thank you, Madam/Mister (whatever their capacity), Toastmasters, guests…"*

Toastmaster of the Day also refers to all roles of the meeting by title: Mr. Timer, Madam Word Master, Madam

Jokemaster, etc. Each of those roles ends his portion of the meeting by saying "Madam/Mister Toastmaster."

If you are a speaker, address the Toastmaster who is in control by saying "Madam/Mister Toastmaster, Toastmasters, guests…"

(Note: As time goes by, many speakers are choosing to eliminate this optional opening and dive right into the speech.)

When you finish speaking, always mention the person from whom you received control of the lectern.

For example:

- If you are the Table Topics Master and completed the Table Topics portion of the meeting, you address the Toastmaster by saying "Madam/Mister Toastmaster." Wait at the lectern until the Toastmaster returns to the lectern.

- If you are a Table Topics Speaker, upon completing your speech, end by saying "Madam/Mister Table Topics Master."

- If you are a speaker, address the Toastmaster who is in control by saying "Madam/Mister Toastmaster." Wait at the lectern until the Toastmaster joins you, shake hands and then be seated.

- If you are the General Evaluator and have just received control from the Toastmaster, address the person who gave you control by saying "Madam/Mister Toastmaster, Toastmasters, guests…," and include Mr. Timer, Madam Grammarian, Mr. Ah Counter, etc.

- If you are an Evaluator, upon completion of your evaluation, end by saying "Madam/Mister General Evaluator."

CHAPTER NINE

Managing Applause

When a person is called to approach the lectern, applaud him from the moment he rises from his seat until he reaches the lectern. It is important that he does not dawdle.

If you are the person in control of the meeting, lead the applause. This helps create a welcoming environment for anyone approaching the lectern.

Never say "I will now turn over the lectern to..." Instead, say "I relinquish control..." or "I return control to...," then shake hands with that person.

CHAPTER TEN

Introducing Dignitaries

Early in the meeting, the President should acknowledge all Toastmasters guest dignitaries in the audience. Guest dignitaries are announced by order of hierarchy: the highest-ranking officer is announced first, and then the others are announced in descending order, for example, Madam Division Director, Mr. Area Director, Mr. President, etc.

Much of the etiquette at a Toastmasters meeting is common sense and courtesy. This basic rule will get you through most situations.

There is a precedence of introductions at a Toastmasters meeting:

- Visiting non-Toastmasters, dignitaries and guests

  - National Government Officials

  - State, Canton or Provincial officials

  - City or Local Officials

  - Special Guest Speakers

  - Prominent Guests

  - Club Guests

  - Current International Officers, Toastmasters

- Current District Officers, in this order:

  - District Director

  - Program Quality Director

  - Club Growth Director

  - Public Relations Manager

  - Administration Manager

  - Finance Manager

  - Logistics Manager

o Immediate Past District Director

- Current Division Directors, in alphabetical order with the "Home" Director taking precedence:

  o Current Area Directors, in area numeric order with the "Home" Director taking precedence

  o Any other current officers, e.g., Presidents from other clubs

  o Past International Directors, starting from the most recent

  o Past District Directors or Governors, starting from the most recent

  o Club members

- An Area Director on an official visit to a club (two per year) takes precedence over officers not present in an official capacity.

When introducing, use the following syntax:

<Office> + <Toastmaster designation in full> + <Name> + <Spouse/partner/guest>

For example, District Director, Distinguished Toastmaster, Rohit Singh and his wife Geetha Singh.

Note that this applies to situations outside the club as well. These are specific forms of formal address for the office, the envelope, the written salutation, the letter ending, in speaking and on the invitation card.

If you host an Ambassador, a Judge, a Bishop or a Datuk, you need to know the correct form of address. This type of protocol is very important when you communicate with government officials or religious dignitaries. The Government Protocol Division or an old-fashioned dictionary may help if you host such personages.

Use your Toastmasters Club as a laboratory for life, and ensure you know what to do. You never know when you will be called upon to perform introductions, so always be prepared.

CHAPTER ELEVEN

Presenting an Award

Whether a club is formerly presenting an educational award or a contest master is presenting trophies and certificates to contest winners, it is critical to make the recipient feel honored. That honor will be bestowed if the correct protocol is followed.

Here are some key Do's and Don'ts when presenting awards:

- Don't bring the person to the lectern before you give his introduction. It can be awkward for him to stand in front of a group while you talk about him, particularly if you speak at any length. Describe the award and the recipient's accomplishments that caused him to deserve the award, then announce the winner and invite him to the stage.

- Don't hand over an unsigned certificate or one with the name left blank. The purpose of an award is to demonstrate the person's value. The message an incomplete certificate sends is "You don't really matter." Send the right message. If you don't know how to spell the name, ask. If you have poor handwriting, find someone else to complete the certificate.

- Don't stand so that the audience can't see you, the recipient or the award. You wouldn't give a speech with your back to your audience or with your props behind your back. Guide the recipient to stand where you can both be seen and the award can be showcased. If there is a camera on hand, be sure to pause at the handshake for the all-important photo opportunity.

- Do make sure you can pronounce the person's name. A person's name is a most valued possession, so treat it as such. If the name is difficult for you, write it out phonetically and then practice, practice, practice!

- Do give the audience some background on the recipient. A little research will make the presentation more meaningful, both to the recipient and to the audience. Learn something about the person receiving the award and share that information in your introduction. Help us get to know the recipient a little better!

- Do hold the award as though it is of high value. Body language is an important part of the presentation. How you hold the award and how you greet the recipient at the lectern convey as much information as what you say. Make eye contact, smile warmly and hand the person the award as though it is a treasure. Treat both the award and the recipient with respect.

- Do read the words on the award. Read every word so the audience understands the impact of the award.

Accepting an Award

Be mentally and physically prepared to acknowledge an award. When accepting, be graceful and brief with your remarks.

If requested to do so, pause for photographs at the lectern or move from the stage area for them.

Minding Your Manners as an Audience Member

There are some key points to remember in your role as an audience member.

Always be respectful and pay attention to anyone at the lectern. Avoid conversations with other audience members during a meeting and do not make unnecessary noises or engage in other distracting activities. Whenever anyone is called to approach the lectern, applaud that person from the moment he rises from his seat until he reaches the lectern. If you are the person in control, lead the applause. This helps create a welcoming environment for speakers standing at the lectern.

Pay attention to the presentation to avoid distracting the speaker. Respect the speaker, even if you disagree with his point of view. Avoid interrupting the speaker with asides and/or comments. If you must leave and/or enter the room, do so during applause or a break in the speech. When the speech/presentation is over, applause should continue until the speaker returns to his seat.

Do's and Don'ts While a Speaker is Speaking

The following fundamentals of good Toastmasters audience behavior are adaptable to virtually any situation:

- Do not talk unless the speaker requests audience participation. If something must be said, whisper it quickly. Excessively shushing a talkative neighbor can be just as disturbing.

- Do not walk in or out of the room while a speaker is speaking.

- Use good posture. Seating is often arranged so that the person in the seat behind can see between the two seats in front, so slumping sideways can block his view.

- Turn off your cell phone, beeper, audible watch and any other sound-making gadgets before a presentation.

- Lights out. Don't forget the screen on your mobile device can be a distraction, too.

Control coughing. Muffle your coughs and sneezes with a handkerchief. Cough drops and mints may be helpful, but leave if you cannot control an attack, preferably between speakers. Avoid other sounds that can disturb the people around you and the performers. Do not munch noisily, smack or crack gum, rattle the pages of programs, tap feet or drum fingers, hum or sing along, rummage in purses—these are just a few of the things that can annoy those around you and be disrespectful to the speaker.

CHAPTER FOURTEEN

Speaking Tips

Here are some valuable tips for speaking:

- Never apologize during a speech.

- Don't turn your back on the audience.

- When leaving the lectern, never cross in front of the next speaker. Walk behind him.

- Use blue note cards instead of white. They are less distracting.

- When using 8-1/2" x 11" sheets for a long presentation at a lectern, slide to the next page rather than flip the page. The audience should not be able to see the pages.

CHAPTER FIFTEEN

Clichés and Crutch Phrases to Avoid

There is no "of" in speakers' titles. For example:

- Sergeant-at-Arms, not Sergeant-of-Arms

- Vice President Education, not Vice President of Education

Avoid the following:

- "Without further ado"

- "At the end of the day"

- "What can I say?"

- "It goes without saying"

- Opening a speech with "So"

- "I've been asked to speak about"

- "Sorry if" or "Sorry for"

- "Excuse the eye chart" (in PowerPoint presentations)

- "I'd like to start out with a story"

- "There's a funny joke"

- "Excuse me if I seem nervous"

- "I'm not good at public speaking"

- "I'm not a speaker"

- "I've never done this before"

- "Bear with me"

- "The next slide shows"

- "Moving right along"

- "I think I've bored you enough"

- "I didn't have enough time"

- "I see the red light, so I'll go through this quickly"

CHAPTER SIXTEEN

Inducting Club Officers

Ideally, an Area Director should preside over a club induction ceremony. However, any officer, Area Director or higher may preside.

Script:

Presiding Officer: Ask current officers to stand. Relieve them of their responsibilities by saying "YOU ARE HEREBY DISCHARGED FROM ALL FURTHER DUTIES AND OFFICERS OF CLUB _____ EFFECTIVE June 30th."

Installation of New Officers – Installing Officer Script

1. Installing Officer: Call the new officers forward as a group to stand in a line to the right of the lectern, with the Sergeant-at-Arms closest to the Installing Officer.

2. Installing Officer: "I am here to install the officers of Club _____ and to prepare them for the challenges that lie ahead. Their collective challenge is to make and keep this Club strong, dedicated to helping people from all walks of life to speak in an effective manner, listen with sensitivity and think creatively. As each officer steps forward, I will ask him or her to hold the gavel as a symbol of leadership."

3. Introduce the Sergeant-at-Arms. As the Sergeant-at-Arms, you are responsible for maintaining club properties, arranging the meeting room and welcoming members and guests at each meeting. Present the gavel as a symbol of this charge. Conclude by saying "WILL YOU PERFORM THESE DUTIES TO THE BEST OF YOUR ABILITY?"

4. Introduce the Secretary. As Secretary, you are responsible for keeping clear and accurate records of club business, including membership records and correspondence with Toastmasters International World Headquarters and others. "WILL YOU PERFORM THESE DUTIES TO THE BEST OF YOUR ABILITY?"

5. Introduce the Treasurer. As Treasurer, you are responsible for keeping clear and accurate financial records of club business and for seeing that the club remains financially stable. "WILL YOU PERFORM THESE DUTIES TO THE BEST OF YOUR ABILITY?"

6. Introduce the Vice President Public Relations. As Vice President Public Relations, you are responsible for coordinating an active public relations and publicity program. Your job is vital to the growth and success of the club, and your efforts help to attract new members. "WILL YOU PERFORM THESE DUTIES TO THE BEST OF YOUR ABILITY?"

7. Introduce Vice President Membership. As Vice President Membership, you are responsible for building membership and ensuring a strong membership base by satisfying the needs of all members. Your efforts contribute to the success of the club. "WILL YOU PERFORM THESE DUTIES TO THE BEST OF YOUR ABILITY?"

8. Introduce the Vice President Education. As Vice President Education, you are responsible for providing and maintaining the positive environment and the programs through which members can learn and grow. If you do your job well, your club will have satisfied members and will continue to grow. "WILL YOU PERFORM THESE DUTIES TO THE BEST OF YOUR ABILITY?"

9. Introduce the President: Having been elected President of Club _____, you are its Chief Executive Officer and will be expected to preside at all Club meetings and at all regular and special meetings of your Executive Committee. As President, you are responsible for providing the supportive club environment members need to fulfill their self-development goals, making sure that members benefit from the Toastmasters Educational Program and helping the club recruit new members and retain current ones. Please accept the gavel as a symbol of your leadership and dedication to office. The gavel is a symbol of the power and authority given to you by the membership of this Club. Use it wisely and with restraint. You are a member of your team as well as a leader. A team is more than a collection of people. It is an emotional force rooted in the feelings, thoughts and actions of all members with the common goal of achievement, sharing and mutual support. Work with your team members to create a healthy, dynamic and Distinguished Club -- a Club of which everyone will be proud. "WILL YOU, AS PRESIDENT, ACCEPT THE CHALLENGE AND PERFORM YOUR DUTIES TO THE BEST OF YOUR ABILITY?" [President answers: "I will."]

10. "Will all the members please stand? The growth and development of the Toastmasters program in Club _____ depends largely upon the actions of this group. On your honor, as men and women of Toastmasters, do you pledge to individually and

collectively stand by this Club, live with it and work with it throughout the coming year?" [Club Members answer: "I will."] Installing Officer wishes the Club well.

11. (Steps 11-13 are optional.) The Immediate Past President and the new President are called to the lectern and exchange the pins of their offices.

12. The new President presents a pin to the Immediate Past President.

13. The new President presents a three-minute speech, outlining the goals and plans for the upcoming term.

CHAPTER SEVENTEEN

Parliamentary Procedure

Every district is required to hold DEC (District Executive Committee) meetings. Although these meetings are to follow parliamentary procedure, many unknowing district leaders are unaware and, thus, speak out of turn, talk over members, and can be disruptive to the meeting.

Most of these disruptions occur during the "making a motion" portion of the DEC meeting. Following is the correct procedure for making a motion.*

*Source: parliamentaryprocedure.net

Motions

In parliamentary procedure the proper way for an individual to propose that the group take a certain action is by "making a motion." The following is the process for handling a motion.

A member addresses the presiding officer for recognition.

The member is recognized.

The member proposes a motion.

Another member must second the motion.

The presiding officer states the motion to the assembly.

The assembly can now discuss or debate the motion. Only one person at a time may speak and must first be recognized by the presiding officer. The presiding officer should try to alternate between those favoring and those opposing the motion.

Preference should be given to:

The person who proposed the motion

A member who has not spoken yet to the motion

A member who seldom speaks to one who frequently addresses the assembly

Discussion must be confined to the question that is "before the house."

The presiding officer takes the vote on the motion. Voting can be done by voice, show of hands or balloting. The presiding officer announces the result of the vote. The floor is now open and another motion can be proposed.

Etiquette from Robert A. Richert, DTM (Used with Permission)

Chris Gregory, DTM, of the Helmsmen Toastmasters in Huntington Beach, California, tells about a meeting where a Toastmaster shocked everyone after his speech. As it happened, this person was the final speaker before a break, and when he was done talking, he abruptly marched out the door. "We all just sat there wondering and waiting," says Gregory. "Thankfully, the president came to the lectern and sent us on the break."

Sound familiar? Incidents like this are not uncommon in most clubs — and it's not always the inexperienced member who abruptly leaves the lectern unattended. Sometimes experienced members become carried away with their thoughts and just walk away.

Some people grip the lectern throughout their talk the way the Peanuts comic-strip character Linus clings to his blanket. In contrast, professional speaker Jack Nichols, DTM, of the Int'l City and Professional Speakers clubs in Southern California, says that others treat the lectern like poison oak. "They will walk around it but not touch it," he notes. "The lectern is not a crutch or a black hole; it is a tool for speakers. I use the lectern at every major presentation."

The manner in which members approach, greet each other, speak at and leave the lectern is important in Toastmasters. Lectern etiquette and use are leadership training tools that teach us discipline, enable us to demonstrate good manners, provide for smooth transitions between program segments and help establish a sense of order. Here are some guidelines to help you properly use the lectern.

First, Lectern or Podium: Which Is It?

In years past, Toastmasters International defined the lectern and podium as two distinct entities: The lectern was the stand that held notes, and the podium was the raised platform on which a speaker would stand. Over the years, however, many metaphorical references to speaking from the podium have altered the usage of these terms so that the distinction is not as sharply defined as before. The Oxford English Dictionary now defines a podium as a raised platform, first, and a lectern, second. It should be noted that this second definition is used mostly in a figurative discussion of a speaker's setting. For the purposes of this article, the original meaning of lectern applies.

Approach the Lectern and Greet Your Host

Once you are introduced, don't spend excessive time approaching the lectern. Avoid making side comments to people along the way. Approach in a confident manner, and shake hands with your host. (Throughout this article, the word host is used as a generic term for the member who introduces speakers, be it the Toastmaster, Topics- master, General Evaluator or whoever else is filling that role.)

If you are carrying materials to the lectern, keep your right hand free so that you can comfortably shake hands. If both hands are full, put the objects down on or near the lectern and then shake hands. Substantial visual aids should be set up before you are introduced — and prior to the meeting, if possible.

Control the Lectern

When you take control of the lectern, you are assuming a leadership role. My Toastmasters mentors used to say, "While at the lectern, a Toastmaster never appears apologetic." They meant that you should be prepared, confident and in charge. Here are some suggested guidelines.

› Once you have greeted the host — and as your host is leaving the lectern — acknowledge him or her with applause. Next, turn to the audience members and greet them. The most commonly used greeting is, "Fellow Toastmasters and honored guests...."

› Set anything you are holding, including a pen, eyeglasses, notes or other objects on the lectern. Unless you intend to begin your speech by displaying one of these potentially distracting items, free your hands before you begin to speak.

› Step back a few inches from the lectern to avoid leaning on it. Next, spread your feet to shoulder width so you won't rock back and forth.

› Do not use the gavel. It is for use only by the president or presiding officer.

› As the host, avoid leaving the lectern unattended. In general, Toastmasters etiquette discourages leaving the lectern unattended. However, certain situations may require you to leave the lectern briefly, for example to help set up visual aids, retrieve an object or in case of an emergency. If you must leave the lectern, always announce your intentions before you go — don't just walk away! If you must leave the lectern for more than a few seconds, declare a brief recess first. Be careful with the terminology: Do not use the word adjourn when you mean recess, because adjourning the meeting means it is over.

Leave the Lectern in Good Hands It is never proper for a member to abruptly leave the lectern after speaking. If you are about to relinquish control of the lectern, always:

› Stay at the lectern until the next person arrives — the host, not the next speaker — to take your place.

› Shake hands with the host, pick up your materials and then relinquish the lectern.

› If you must cross paths with the host who has just approached, step back and walk behind the host. Never walk in front of the member taking control of the lectern.

› Walk directly back to your seat. Use the lectern properly to increase meeting efficiency, help foster a professional atmosphere and promote leadership training.

Robert A. Richert, DTM, also provided some great information in the article titled "Mind Your Lectern Manners" on page 22 of the February 2012 issue of Toastmaster magazine.

Do you grip the lectern throughout your talk like the Peanuts comic-strip character Linus clings to his blanket? Do you treat the lectern like poison oak walking around it but not touching it? The lectern is not a crutch or black hole. Use it as a tool for speakers.

If you carry materials to the lectern, keep your right hand free so that you can comfortably shake hands. If both hands are full, put the objects down on or near the lectern and then shake hands. Set aside anything you are holding. Unless you intend to begin your speech by holding something, free your hands before you begin to speak.

Step back a few inches from the lectern to avoid leaning on it. Next, spread your feet to shoulder width so you won't rock back and forth. It's never proper for a member to abruptly leave the lectern after speaking. Stay at the lectern until the next person arrives – the host. Shake hands with the host, pick up your materials, and then relinquish the lectern.

If you must cross paths with the host who has just approached, step back and walk behind the host. Then walk directly back to your seat. Use the lectern properly to increase meeting efficiency, help foster a professional atmosphere, and promote leadership training.

Next Success Steps

As leaders, we all strive to set an example of professionalism regardless of our role. The proper use of meeting etiquette is a key part of being the role model and example for others.

Practice and share these tips with those who are looking to truly lead from the lectern with both poise and professionalism.

If the information in this short book is new to you, use this handy guide as often as possible until meeting etiquette becomes second nature to you. If you have any suggestions, comments or questions, please email them to me at SharonAnitaHill@icloud.com. I am always open to ways to make this guide more effective for all Toastmaster leaders.

About the Author

Sharon Anita Hill, DTM, author, speaker and MBA, spent more than 20 years as a development and marketing manager at Fortune 500 giant IBM. As a Toastmasters International district award winner, Sharon displays mastery and confidence speaking for audiences ranging in size from 10 to 500+.

Sharon Hill teaches, writes, speaks and coaches individuals and companies about the skills necessary to become grounded in all human interactions while leveraging the advantages of technology. She offers learning combined with a keen sense of humor to enhance and complement each experience.

As a Certified Etiquette Trainer (CET), Sharon uses the breakthrough formulas created by the American Business Etiquette Trainers Association (ABETA) to teach employees and students how to always present themselves as poised, professional, and confident. She's an acclaimed Toastmaster and former member of the National Speakers Association. Sharon is also a Certified Communicator from Duke University and a radio talk show host.

Through her time–tested experience, Sharon Hill offers her etiquette hints and tips to help companies succeed in business today. Her energy, enthusiasm and humor delight her diverse audiences as they experience her rapid-learning formulas for success.

Sharon also finds time to extend her passion for etiquette as an author, workshop leader, corporate trainer and keynote speaker. She has written four books on etiquette, succeeding in college and corporate America. To learn more about Sharon and her work, visit www.sharonhillinternational.com.